# Experience

Three One-Act Plays
About
Ralph Waldo Emerson


by

Stephen Evans

For production permissions and rights, contact:
info@timebeingmedia.com

Cover photo: The Old North Bridge in Concord, Massachusetts. Photo by Stephen Evans.

Experience: Second Edition

ISBN: 9781953725738

Time Being Media LLC

"Grief too will make us idealists.

Ralph Waldo Emerson
*Experience*, 1842

STEPHEN EVANS

STEPHEN EVANS

# Monuments

STEPHEN EVANS

# The History

"I visited Ellen's tomb & opened the coffin."

Ralph Waldo Emerson
*Journal Entry March 29, 1832*

In July of 1872, Ralph Waldo Emerson's house in Concord, Massachusetts, caught fire. His many friends and admirers raised money for repairs, and to send him on a journey across the ocean while those repairs were being made.

At the time of this voyage, Emerson was one of the most famous Americans in the world, and the most famous American intellectual since Benjamin Franklin. Everywhere he went he was invited to speak and read from his works. But his memory, which had been declining for a few years, declined even more seriously after the fire. No longer considered capable of traveling alone, his daughter Ellen Tucker Emerson (who was named after his first wife) accompanied him and managed the trip.

This tale of a few moments on that voyage is imagined, though based in some details on the letters of Emerson's first wife Ellen, his namesake daughter Ellen, and his journals.

# Cast of Characters

WALDO          Ralph Waldo Emerson, age 69

NELLY          Emerson's Daughter Ellen, age 33[1],
               referred to as Nelly in this play
               because the playwright was getting
               confused.

ELLEN          Emerson's first wife, Ellen, age 21[1]

# Scene

A boat on the River Nile.

# Time

1873.

---

[1] May be played by the same actress.

# ACT I SCENE 1

**Setting:**   Emerson's cabin. Downstage right is a desk, chair behind, so the actor faces the audience. Up left is a doorway. Downstage from that is a window of sorts.

**At Rise:**   Waldo is at his desk. He is struggling to light an oil lamp.

NELLY
Let there be light.

NELLY
*From offstage*
Papa, you should come out on deck. You can see the pyramids.

WALDO
I imagine they will last until the return trip.

*Nelly enters.*

NELLY
What are you working on, Papa?

WALDO
Genesis.

*She laughs.*

NELLY
Can you be more specific?

WALDO
Chapter 1, verse 3.

*He fiddles with the lamp.*

NELLY
Are you writing about it?

WALDO
No, I am re-enacting it.

*He fiddles some more, without success, then
throws up his hands.*

WALDO
Let there be light!

*She moves to the desk and lights the lamp for
him.*

NELLY
There. Now you can call the light day.

WALDO
*Squinting*
I would call this dim not day.

NELLY
And set about dividing the darkness from the light.

WALDO
Wishful thinking, daughter.

NELLY
As you have always done, Papa.

*She kisses his forehead and looks at the desk.*

NELLY
What are you working on today instead of talking a stroll on deck with your devoted daughter?

WALDO
Plutarch's Morals. I wish Henry were here. He knew the Greeks so much better than I.

*Ellen is struck with sadness, her brilliant father's decline brought home again, as it is many times each day.*

NELLY
He is gone, Papa. Henry Thoreau died ten years ago.

*Waldo stops, confused and then struggles to remember, accepts, then tries to cover his struggle.*

*Nelly, ever the loving daughter, waits patiently for his mind to catch up.*

WALDO
Then I change my mind. I don't wish he were here. He would be annoyed with me for disturbing his lecture to the Almighty.

*Nelly laughs, but the sadness shows through.*

NELLY
You are a wise man.

*Waldo, all too aware of his decline, smiles.*

WALDO
So everyone tells me.

NELLY
Do you doubt it, O Sage of Concord?

WALDO
Among many things.

*Nelly tries to change the subject.*

NELLY
I thought Plutarch was a Roman.

WALDO
No. He was a citizen of the Empire, but he was Greek by birth, and by thought.

NELLY
Plutarch was one of my favorites as a child. When you were away on your lecture tours, I would sneak into your study and read him.

WALDO
You were a precocious child. I credit your mother with that. I was away so often. Did you read the Lives?

NELLY
No. Too stuffy, too many wars. I liked the Morals actually. Is this Professor Goodwin's translation?

WALDO

Yes. Saved from the fire. I am to write the introduction and must have it ready soon.

*Again, the sadness hits her. She gathers herself, crosses back to the desk, and lays her hand on his shoulder with great tenderness.*

NELLY

That is already done, Papa.

*She turns to the front of the book.*

NELLY

*Reading*

With an introduction by Ralph Waldo Emerson.

*Waldo looks at the book, confused. He turns a few pages. Then turns a few back, always the familiar struggle to comprehend, catch up with the world.*

WALDO

It is done.

*Another pause.*

Wonderful!

*He relaxes.*

Oh I am quite relieved. I was dreading the labor. The words do not flow as easily these days.

*He shakes it off, returning to a familiar quotation to explain the lapse.*

But who cares? As soon as we walk out of doors,
Nature transcends all poets so far, that a little more or
less skill in whistling is of no account.[2]

> *Nelly understands, glances outside, then at him,*
> *and takes charge, as she has so often done and*
> *will continue to do for the rest of his life.*

> NELLY

Papa, come out of this stuffy cabin and we'll find
chairs in the sun and watch the ages float past us.

> *He smiles at her, grateful for her concern and her*
> *care.*

> *The smile fades.*

> *He looks around the cabin, again deep in*
> *confusion.*

> WALDO

This is a boat.

> NELLY

Yes, Papa.

> *Waldo tries to solve the puzzle.*

> WALDO

Not on the ocean.

---

[2] From a letter to Caroline Sturgis, Oct. 23, 1857

NELLY

No.

WALDO

A river?

NELLY

Yes.

WALDO

A river.

NELLY

Yes.

*He looks out the window.*

WALDO

The Concord?

NELLY

No.

WALDO

No. Too large. Nor the Charles either.

NELLY

It is the Nile.

*Pause.*

WALDO

The Nile?

NELLY

We are in Egypt, Papa. We are sailing down the Nile on a boat named the Aurora. Remember how shocked we were at the price? Eight dollars a day.

*Slowly it dawns and he catches up.*

WALDO

Yes. I remember now. Can we afford such extravagance?

*She puts a hand on his shoulder.*

NELLY

We can. Remember the fire?

WALDO

The fire. Yes! The fire.

NELLY

The fire burned our house.

WALDO

Yes. Yes. Our poor home.

NELLY

Then your friends and many admirers raised the money to send us on this trip while it is restored.

*He is lost in thought for a moment. Then he notices the book in front of him and turns back to it, something solid he understands.*

WALDO

According to Plutarch, the Egyptians invented horticulture.

NELLY

And slavery.

WALDO

The Egyptians did not invent slavery. They merely perfected it.

NELLY

That I thought was an American accomplishment.

WALDO

Now, now. Mr. Lincoln fixed all that.

NELLY[3]

Papa, surely you don't think—

*She sees him smiling.*

Yes, you know me well.

*Nelly picks up the volume, flips through.*

NELLY

I loved these stories. Especially...

*She finds the one she wants.*

Isis and Osiris. I used to read this one over and over.

---

[3] Ellen, her mother Lidian, Henry Thoreau, and about half of Concord were staunch abolitionists and initially supporters of John Brown. Emerson, though not as personally passionate, sometimes lent his famous name to the cause.

WALDO
That is hardly a story for children!

NELLY[4]
Exactly why I loved it! It is the oldest love story in the world. Osiris was entombed by Typhon and thrown into the sea and Isis searched all over the world for him and opened the coffin and took out the body and laid her cheek against his and then Typhon found the body and cut it up into pieces and threw it into the Nile and Isis searched the river and found every piece except—

WALDO
Yes. Yes. I know the story.

NELLY
For a young girl, it was scandalous. And very romantic.

*Waldo gazes out the window.*

WALDO
It happened here, if it happened. Thousands of years ago. The tomb of Osiris is on the island of—

NELLY
Philae[5].

WALDO
Philae, which lies...

---

[4] Ellen never married, living in her father's house for the rest of her life, an adoring aunt to her sibling's children.
[5] Pronounced Fi-Lee

NELLY
Not far ahead of us.

*Philae reminds Waldo of something. He starts to drift away into memory.*

WALDO
I have wanted to see Philae for many years.

NELLY
The captain tells me that the Wards are there, with Clover Adams[6].

WALDO
Many many years.

NELLY
I arranged transportation for us on Philae so we may join them straightaway.

*He pauses, then comes back. He turns to Nelly, takes her hands, and looks at her approvingly.*

WALDO
You remind me of your mother, Ellen.

*She brushes the white hair away from his forehead.*

NELLY
I was named for her, Papa. But your first wife Ellen was not my mother.

---

[6] Wife of Henry Adams and the inspiration for some of Henry James characters.

*He laughs.*

WALDO

I am forgetful now I know. But that I have not forgotten. Your mother Lidian is the best woman, the best wife. She deserves...she deserves...you. You should be home helping her restore our home, not running away to foreign lands with your old Papa.

*Waldo stares at his hands.*

NELLY

Don't think of that now. There will be time enough for setting things right when we return home. If mother and Edith have not already done so.

WALDO

If anyone can, it is...Lidian. She is...the best woman, the best wife.

NELLY

Papa?

WALDO

Yes?

NELLY

I often wonder...

WALDO

As do I. In the blood I suppose. The wandering wondering Emersons.

NELLY

I often wonder, I was saying.

WALDO
If you are saying, you might as well say.

NELLY
I often wonder how you managed to convince Mother to name me after your first wife. And not just one name. She was Ellen Tucker Emerson. I am Ellen Tucker Emerson.

WALDO
You have wondered that?

NELLY
Can you blame me?

WALDO
I suppose not. Best ask your mother.

NELLY
I have. She said to ask you.

WALDO
Did she?

NELLY
She did. I think she was curious what your answer would be.

WALDO
So am I.

NELLY
I would like to know. If you remember.

WALDO
While I remember, you mean.

NELLY
You must have been quite persuasive. Even for Ralph
Waldo Emerson.

WALDO
I suppose it was my idea. Back then I had that much
audacity, and that little understanding of women. But
your mother agreed.

NELLY
Apparently. But why?

WALDO
My first wife and I were married not even two years
before she died, and she was ill with the consumption
so much of that. I think we knew before we married.

NELLY
Knew what?

WALDO
That we had not much time.

*He is lost in thought again. Then, again, returns
to the book.*

WALDO
I wish Henry were here. He knew the Greeks so much
better than I.

*Nelly sighs.*

NELLY
I shall be on deck, Papa, riddling the sphinx. Join me.

*Nelly exits.*

WALDO
One monument to another, eh?

*He continues to turn pages, then finally finds what he wants.*

WALDO
*Reading*
With an introduction by Ralph Waldo Emerson.

*He turns a few pages.*

WALDO
*Reading*
Plutarch's popularity will return in rapid cycles. If over-read in this decade, so that his anecdotes and opinions become commonplace, and to-day's novelties are sought for variety, his sterling values will presently recall the eye and thought of the best minds, and his books will be reprinted and read anew by coming generations. And thus Plutarch will be perpetually rediscovered from time to time as long as books last.[7]

*He closes the book.*

---

[7] *Plutarch's Morals, with an Introduction by Ralph Waldo Emerson*

WALDO

It is finished. I didn't know. I didn't remember. But how can one know what has been forgotten? Is there some sign? An empty space where memories used to be? Like a piece missing from a puzzle?

*He sighs.*

WALDO

I should like to know what I don't know. Even if that is the only thing I can know.

*He opens the book again, turns the pages more and more rapidly, almost desperately, then finally finds what he wants.*

WALDO

*Reading*

And in the first place where she could take rest, and found herself to be now at liberty and alone, she opened the ark, and laid her cheeks upon the cheeks of Osiris, and embraced him and wept bitterly[8].

ELLEN (V.O.)

We knew.

*This voice, almost whispered. He can almost remember it.*

WALDO

We knew?

---

[8] *Of Isis and Osiris*, Plutarch's Morals

ELLEN (V.O.)
That we had not much time.

*More familiar.*

WALDO
Did we?

ELLEN (V.O.)
We spoke of it.

*Waldo closes the book. He knows, but cannot believe.*

WALDO
I do not believe in the immortality of the individual soul.

ELLEN (OFF)
Since when?

*He stands. The light grows around him.*

WALDO
Since I lost you.

*He turns upstage. Ellen is revealed upstage, wearing her funeral dress. Her face is covered by a veil.*

ELLEN
You never lost me.

WALDO
I couldn't find you.

ELLEN
It's not the same.

WALDO
Nothing is.

ELLEN
Nothing is.

*Ellen crosses down into the light.*

ELLEN
Anyway I'm not a ghost or a spirit or a lost soul. I'm a memory.

WALDO
Well then I suppose you can stay. There is plenty of room. Most of the other memories have left. And they took yesterday with them.

ELLEN
You haven't forgotten me, have you, Waldo? Have you forgotten your Ellinelli? Your Lady Frolick? Lady Pensero? Have you forgotten your queen, my king?

WALDO
Facts fade. Feelings remain.

ELLEN
You can't have forgotten everything. Else I would not be here.

WALDO
How can one know?

ELLEN

A puzzle. But then you like puzzles.

WALDO

Do I?

ELLEN

I hope so. I am one.

*She laughs. He smiles at the sound.*

WALDO

That is familiar.

ELLEN

Shall I remind you?

WALDO

Yes. Remind me. Please. Re*mind* me.

ELLEN

We met on Christmas day. You were my favorite gift.
I was a woman of 16 and you were a boy of 24. We
spoke of Byron. You thought I meant the poet and I
thought you meant my spaniel. We were very
confused for a moment, and then your stern and
serious ministerial face crinkled up and you laughed
and laughed. And I decided then and there that you
would marry me.

WALDO

You had a dog named Byron.

ELLEN

That you remember! I would be insulted but he was a
very good dog.

WALDO

Byron. Funny.

ELLEN

A year later you brought me a book called *Forget Me Not*. A year! Now that is funny.

WALDO

That is ironic. It's not the same.

ELLEN

What is ironic is that I grew up in Concord, New Hampshire, and after I died you settled in Concord, Massachusetts.

WALDO

That is not ironic. It is a coincidence, and possibly a metaphor.

ELLEN

I wanted to be a poet and you wanted to be a minister. You ended up a poet and I ended up a memory. What is that?

WALDO

That is a tragedy.

ELLEN

Oh, your poetry is not that bad.

*He looks at her.*

WALDO

That is funny.

*She curtsies.*

ELLEN

Are they coming back?

WALDO

What?

ELLEN

The memories.

WALDO

Oh they come back occasionally. They just don't stay.
Memories are like some old aunt who goes in and out
of the house, and occasionally recites anecdotes of old
times and persons which I recognize as having heard
before, and she being gone again I search in vain for
any trace.[9]

ELLEN

That sounds like something you wrote.

WALDO

I don't recall.

ELLEN

Shall I?

WALDO

What?

ELLEN

Stay?

*He looks offstage where Nelly has exited.*

---

[9] *Essay on Memory*, Emerson

WALDO
Ellen is...out there.

ELLEN
I am Ellen.

WALDO
You are Ellinelli. You are Lady Frolick and Lady Pensero.

ELLEN
I believe so.

WALDO
I remember something that I have forgotten.

ELLEN
You had forgotten but now you remember?

WALDO
No, I remember that I have forgotten.

ELLEN
I see.

WALDO
I have tried and tried.

ELLEN
Yes?

WALDO
For some time, I have tried.

ELLEN
Yes?

WALDO

I cannot recall.

ELLEN

Say it.

WALDO

Your face. I cannot recall your face.

ELLEN

Is that all?

WALDO

I want to. Very much. But I cannot.

ELLEN

I'm almost glad. I was not so beautiful toward the end.
So pale and thin.

WALDO

You were always beautiful.

ELLEN

But wait. You have my miniature still?

WALDO

Your picture. Yes. I have it in my study. Or I did. Who
knows where it is now? I don't think it burned.
Though that night was so confusing.

ELLEN

Poor Waldo.

WALDO

That I remember. You called me that often.

ELLEN

If you have the miniature, then you can't have forgotten how I looked.

WALDO

I look at the painting. Often. But I do not recognize you when I see it.

ELLEN

Was it not a good likeness?

WALDO

It's not that. It just doesn't feel the same.

ELLEN

The same?

WALDO

As when I looked at you. I still remember the way I felt. Transcendent.

ELLEN

Transcendent? You make me sound very grand.

WALDO

You were.

ELLEN

Transcendent? No. I was a girl in love, for the first and only time. You mistake transcendent for incandescent.

*Her lighting brightens a bit.*

WALDO

Transcendent sounds better.

ELLEN

You're just used to it[10].

WALDO

Perhaps.

ELLEN

I suppose I was a little transcendent, towards the end.
It was so hard to hold on to life. I tried, for you.

WALDO

You were brave. I remember that.

ELLEN

We had so little time. I didn't want to waste it in tears.

WALDO

And your cough. Your terrible cough. And the blood.
So much blood from such a tiny body.

ELLEN

I am healed now.

WALDO

I took you south, to try the climate.

ELLEN

To Philadelphia!

WALDO

And I had to leave you there and return to Boston. I
have never felt so alone.

---

[10] Emerson was the 'founder' of American
Transcendentalism.

ELLEN
I was the one in Philadelphia.

WALDO
And I was desperate to know if you missed me as
much as I missed you.

ELLEN
That is natural. You were so young.

WALDO
Natural. You were young. Was I ever young?

ELLEN
You were. You just didn't know it.

WALDO
I feel younger now, with you here.

ELLEN
Dear Waldo.

WALDO
Dear Waldo. I remember that, now, too. No one else
has ever called me that. Lidian calls me Mr. Emerson.
May I speak of her to you?

ELLEN
Sweet Waldo.

WALDO
I know she has never called me that. Not in my
hearing anyway.

ELLEN
You love her.

WALDO

It is, imprecise, to use the same word for what I felt
for you, and what I feel for her. But it is the only word
we are given. Even Shakespeare never found another.
So I suppose we must make the best of it.

ELLEN

But this dream of love, though beautiful, is only one
scene in our play. In the procession of the soul from
within outward, it enlarges its circles ever, like the
pebble thrown into the pond, or the light proceeding
from an orb.[11]

WALDO

That sounds like something I once wrote.

ELLEN

It is.

WALDO

If you are a memory, how is it that you know
something I wrote years after.

ELLEN

Memories don't abide alone. We coexist.

WALDO

Really?

ELLEN

Oh yes. We speak to one another often.

---

[11] *Essay on Love*, Emerson

WALDO
Memories speak to memories.

ELLEN
Well, think of it. What else is there to do but speak to each other? Especially when you spend so little time with us. Such a busy important man, always running around giving speeches.

WALDO
Lectures, not speeches. Politicians give speeches.

*She sticks her tongue out at him through the veil, laughs, spinning away, her white dress flowing around her. She stops, then turns slyly back to Waldo.*

ELLEN
In fact, Lidian and I have spoken.

WALDO
Pardon?

ELLEN
Lidian. Your second wife. You member her, don't you?

WALDO
Oh yes.

ELLEN
I thought so. Lidian and I have had long conversations.

WALDO
About me?

ELLEN

Oh yes!

WALDO

Oh no.

ELLEN

And she does call you poor Mr. Emerson, if that is any consolation.

WALDO

For a memory, you are very chatty.

ELLEN

Memories are not miniatures.

WALDO

What are they? I don't remember.

ELLEN

Memory is a presumption of a possession of the future. Now we are halves, we see the past but not the future, but in that day will the hemisphere complete itself and foresight be as perfect as aftersight.[12]

WALDO

Or as imperfect. Did I write that?

ELLEN

Of course.

WALDO

It is like your face. Though I know it, I don't recognize it.

---

[12] *Essay on Memory*, Emerson

ELLEN

I like that one especially. It reminds me of your sermons. One of the saddest parts of being sick was that I could not attend your sermons.

WALDO

It reminds you?

ELLEN

You were so grand in the pulpit with your high cloak and sweet voice. And only once per sermon would you let yourself sneak a glance at your Ellinelli. And when you did look on my face, only for a second and with no smile or nod or sign, I knew I needed no other communion.

WALDO

Nor I.

*He turns suddenly.*

WALDO

I remember!

*Ellen turns away.*

ELLEN

My face?

WALDO

For a year afterwards, I walked each day to your grave.

*He turns to her.*

ELLEN

Poor Waldo.

WALDO

You asked me to.

ELLEN

Did I?

WALDO

Breathe not yet, but wait until
My spirit is set free.
Then whisper round my grave
The tale of my release −[13]

ELLEN

I wrote that.

WALDO

You did.

ELLEN

And you remember.

WALDO

I do.

ELLEN

But you cannot recall my face.

WALDO

No. I remember I walked each day to your grave.

*He takes a step toward her.*

---

[13] *To the South Wind*, Ellen Emerson

> WALDO

I needed to see your face. Once more.

*Another step. Dimmer.*

> WALDO

Just once more.

*Another step, and he is near her.*

> WALDO

One day I entered your tomb.

*She turns to him.*

> WALDO

And opened the coffin.

*He reaches up to her veil.*

> WALDO

And I saw.

*Her light goes out. He lowers his arm.*

> WALDO

Nothing.

> ELLEN

Nothing?

> WALDO

Nothing.

> ELLEN

It was empty?

WALDO
We were in darkness.

ELLEN
That is natural.

WALDO
Natural. Yes. Does it bother you?

ELLEN
What?

WALDO
That I, came to see you?

ELLEN
I often come to see you.

WALDO
Are you sure you are not a ghost?

ELLEN
Maybe a memory is a ghost that lives inside us.

WALDO
Maybe a ghost is a memory that lives outside us.

ELLEN
But you don't believe in the immortality of the soul.

WALDO
Maybe that is where memories go. The afterlife
belongs not to us but to them.

*She steps into the light again.*

ELLEN

Perhaps they are us.

WALDO

After you died, I resigned from the ministry. Your inheritance paid for long trip through Europe. I was lost, so I thought I may as well be lost somewhere new.

ELLEN

Clever Waldo.

WALDO

That's a new one. I wandered for a year. Syracuse. Naples. Rome. Florence. Paris. London.

ELLEN

So far from home.

WALDO

Without you I had no home.

ELLEN

So far then.

WALDO

I met great writers that I had admired: Landor, Coleridge, Wordsworth, Carlyle.

ELLEN

Your Heroes.

WALDO

I found them to be...just men. Poor men. Flawed men.

ELLEN

You were disappointed.

WALDO

Yes. But. It is a kind of freedom, to learn what is possible, and by whom.

ELLEN

It is.

WALDO

By the end I knew something in me had changed, but I did not know what.

ELLEN

I know.

WALDO

I came back, to Concord. I could not return to Boston and the church.

ELLEN

I understand.

WALDO

I had to make a living, so I started writing, and speaking.

*She smiles.*

ELLEN

Lecturing.

*And he smiles.*

WALDO
Lecturing. I married Lidian.

ELLEN
A good woman.

WALDO
A good woman.

ELLEN
You needed her.

WALDO
I loved her. Love her. You can tell her I said so.

ELLEN
You can tell her.

WALDO
I can tell her.

ELLEN
She gave you children.

WALDO
Ellen. Edith. Edward. Poor Waldo, gone so young.[14]

ELLEN
Poor Waldo. So much tragedy.

WALDO
So much life.

ELLEN
If I had not gotten sick...

---

[14] Emerson's son Waldo died of scarlet fever at age five.

WALDO
I could not have left you.

ELLEN
Maybe that is why I had to leave you.

WALDO
Let us build altars to the Beautiful Necessity. [15]

ELLEN
Though thou loved her as thyself,
As a self of purer clay,
Though her parting dims the day,
Stealing grace from all alive; [16]

WALDO
Heartily know,
When half-gods go,
The gods arrive. [17]

ELLEN
It's all right.

WALDO
I remember.

ELLEN
The loving. And the leaving. It is all right.

---

[15] *Essay on Experience*, Emerson
[16] *Give All to Love*, poem, Emerson

### WALDO

Silent rushes the swift Lord
Through ruined systems still restored,
Broad-sowing, bleak and void to bless,
Plants with worlds the wilderness,
Waters with tears of ancient sorrow
Apples of Eden ripe to-morrow;
House and tenant go to ground.[17]

### ELLEN

Lost in God.[18]

### WALDO

In Godhead found.[18]

*He returns to the desk.*

### WALDO

I have wondered from time to time what my last
memory will be. After all the others have escaped me.
What will be the last? Like Pandora's box, my mind
will shut tight, yet one will tap on the lid and cry out
'wait! I am still here.'

*He looks to Ellen.*

### WALDO

Will it be you? Lidian? Nelly? Henry? Little Waldo
feverish in the bed? What will it be? What part of
myself will be the last to say goodbye?

---

[17] *Threnody*, poem, Emerson

ELLEN

It may be a bit selfish but I should like it to be me. But it won't be.

*She starts to exit.*

ELLEN

It won't be me. Or Lidian. Or Nelly. Or Henry. Or little Waldo. For you it will be a boat on river in a land where history waits.

WALDO

I have lived two lives. One of the mind. One of the heart. The mind is leaving. Only the heart remains.

*She turns back to him. He looks at her.*

WALDO

One monument to another.

*The light slowly fades.*

**The End**

# Solid Seasons

STEPHEN EVANS

# The History

*"There was one other with whom I had "solid seasons,"*
*long to be remembered, at his house in the village, and*
*who looked in upon me from time to time."*

Henry David Thoreau,

*Walden*

In September of 1847, after two productive and life-altering years in his cabin at Walden Pond, Henry David Thoreau left Walden and eventually returned to the household of his friend and mentor Ralph Waldo Emerson.

Why did he leave?

In Walden, Thoreau says:

"I left the woods for as good a reason as I went there. Perhaps it seemed to me that I had several more lives to live, and could not spare any more time for that one."

STEPHEN EVANS

# Cast of Characters

**WALDO**       Ralph Waldo Emerson

**HENRY**       Henry David Thoreau

# Setting

Thoreau's cabin at Walden Pond.

# Time

July 4th, 1847.

# ACT I SCENE 1

**Setting**:     Thoreau's cabin.

**At Rise**:     HENRY is at his table. He is struggling
to light an oil lamp.

HENRY
Let there be light.

*WALDO knocks and enters.*

WALDO
Hello Henry. How are the beans?

HENRY
Welcome Mr. Emerson. Beans?

WALDO
Mrs. Emerson has sent me for some beans.

*Pause.*

HENRY
Beans.

WALDO
Beans?

*Henry nods. This is a game they play, but
beneath the play, the competition between them
is only barely hidden.*

*Waldo thinks.*

WALDO
Pounding beans is good to the end of pounding empires one of these days; but if, at the end of years, it is still only beans![18]

HENRY
Ha!

*Henry picks up a piece of paper and reads.*

HENRY
The same sun which ripens my beans illumines at once a system of earths like ours.[19]

*Waldo nods.*

WALDO
You.

*Henry nods. Waldo points to the paper.*

WALDO
Is that new?

HENRY
It is. A book I think. Maybe a lecture. But I think it's a book.

WALDO
About?

---

[18] Emerson. *Eulogy of Thoreau*
[19]. Thoreau, *Walden*

HENRY
Me I suppose.

WALDO
You?

HENRY
Yes.

WALDO
You're writing about you?

HENRY
Franklin did it. Rousseau did it.

WALDO
Of course Henry. Of course.

HENRY
Even you have done it, Mr. Emerson.

WALDO
When?

HENRY
In your essay on Experience. You wrote about little
Waldo. How you felt when he. When he got sick.

WALDO
Yes. Yes. But. That was to illustrate a point. I wasn't
writing about myself.

HENRY
I am doing the same. Just on a slightly larger scale.

WALDO
What point are you illustrating?

HENRY
I'm not sure yet.

WALDO
I see.

HENRY
It's a work in progress.

WALDO
Aren't they all?

HENRY
It's about...my time here.

WALDO
DaVinci said that art is never finished.

HENRY
What I have learned.

WALDO
L'arte non è mai Finita.

HENRY
What?

WALDO
DaVinci. That's what he said. I thought you knew
Italian, Henry.

HENRY
Italian? Yes. A bit. French. Latin. Spanish. German.
Greek.

WALDO
And your English is coming along well too.

HENRY
Is it? Praise from Ralph Waldo Emerson himself.
What more could one ask?

WALDO
You have so much promise Henry. I don't want you to
waste it.

*Henry holds up a sheaf of papers.*

HENRY
I am transforming my journal into a book.

*Waldo smiles.*

WALDO
Now where did you learn that?

HENRY
I wonder.

*Henry puts down the papers, looks around the
cabin.*

HENRY
I'm thinking of calling it Life in the Woods.

WALDO
These are hardly the woods, Henry.

*Henry smiles.*

HENRY
It is a domestic wilderness.

WALDO

Henry, you know I dislike it when you do that. It is a rhetorical trick of which you are much too fond.

*Henry smiles more broadly.*

HENRY

I know.

*Now Waldo smiles.*

WALDO

Ha. Anyway, you're a mile from the town common.

*Henry pauses. Back to the game.*

HENRY

Common.

*Waldo takes his time. Then.*

WALDO

Nothing astonishes men so much as common sense and plain dealing.[20]

*Henry picks up his sheath of papers again.*

HENRY

If one advances confidently in the direction of his dreams, and endeavors to live the life which he has imagined, he will meet with a success unexpected in common hours.[21]

---

[20] Emerson, *Art*
[21] Thoreau, *Walden*

*They pause.*

*Waldo nods.*

WALDO
You again.

HENRY
Yours was good though.

WALDO
Thank you. I'll have to try and remember it.

*Waldo takes the sheath of papers from Henry.*

*He peruses them.*

*Mumbling.*

*Nodding.*

*Scowling.*

*Henry gets nervous.*

HENRY
The town common is a mile and three quarters.

WALDO
*(Not looking up)*
You are the surveyor. I bow to your superior
knowledge.
*(Now he looks up)*
As to distance.

*Henry smiles.*

HENRY
You don't like the title Life in the Woods?

WALDO
Simple titles, Henry. One word if possible. Nature.
Experience.  Self-Reliance.

HENRY
That's two words.

WALDO
It's hyphenated. Counts as one.

HENRY
I bow to your superior knowledge. As to hyphens.

*Waldo sits and glances around the cabin.*

WALDO
Anyway, why are you working on something new? I
thought you were still reworking the other one. The
river book.

HENRY
A Week on the Concord and Merrimack Rivers.

WALDO
Short titles, Henry. Short titles.

WALDO
I'll try to remember, Mr. Emerson.

WALDO

And three names. If you have them. Ralph Waldo
Emerson. David Henry Thoreau. It adds gravity. We
all need a little gravity.

HENRY

Henry David. You forget I changed it.

WALDO

Ah yes. Henry David Thoreau. That does sound
better. Perhaps I should have done that. Waldo Ralph
Emerson?

*Pause while they consider, then look at each
other.*

BOTH

No.

WALDO

When you have Ralph and Waldo to choose from, I
suppose it makes no difference.

HENRY

Emerson has a solid ring to it.

WALDO

Do you think?

HENRY

Oh yes.

WALDO

Perhaps. Perhaps you are just used to it.

HENRY

No one can pronounce Thoreau. They always put the accent on the second syllable.

WALDO

It is better to be famously mispronounced than pronounced infamous.

*Henry pauses. Repeats the phrase to himself.*

HENRY

That makes no sense.

*Waldo pauses. Repeats the phrase to himself.*

WALDO

True. It sounds good though.

HENRY

Fame is not something I shall ever know.

WALDO

It was not something I expected when I was a young minister in Boston. But here we are. Though some would say I am more infamous than famous.

HENRY

Ha.

WALDO

First the publication of my little Nature book, which caused so much ruckus. Then my Divinity School disaster.

HENRY

It was a fine speech.

WALDO
Lecture. Politicians give speeches.

HENRY
Sorry.

WALDO
They still won't allow me to speak there.

HENRY
Lecture. See I do listen.

*Waldo laughs.*

WALDO
Still.

HENRY
They don't know you.

WALDO
That is what fame is. Being widely unknown.

HENRY
That makes sense. I just can't quite figure out why.

WALDO
Fame.

*Henry thinks.*

HENRY
Rather than love, than money, than fame, give me truth.[22]

---

[22] Thoreau, *Walden*

WALDO

All the toys that infatuate men, and which they play for,—houses, land, money, luxury, power, fame, are the selfsame thing, with a new gauze or two of illusion overlaid. [23]

*They pause, thinking.*

HENRY

You.

WALDO

I don't know. Yours has a power mine lacks, a straightforwardness. It reminds me of the way I used to write.

HENRY

A young man's phrase, you're saying. You think I will grow out of it?

WALDO

I hope not. I would write that way still if I could. If I still had that confidence. That clarity.

*Waldo picks up a paper on the desk.*

WALDO

Your essay on Thomas Carlyle? It was published?

HENRY

It was. Though Mr. Greely is having trouble getting me paid for it.

---

[23] Emerson, *Fate*

WALDO
Lectures, Henry. That is what the public wants. And you get paid in advance.

HENRY
You do.

WALDO
Your lecture on Mr. Carlyle was well received. Many of our friends remarked on it.

HENRY
I don't think lecturing is for me.

WALDO
Why not?

HENRY
I can't say what I think.

WALDO
Since when? I have never known you to hold back your opinions. On anything.

*Henry nods, and smiles.*

HENRY
We have that in common.

WALDO
I suppose we do.

HENRY
People don't like me.

WALDO
Everyone likes you Henry. It's just.

HENRY

Yes?

WALDO

They don't understand you. You read all these
languages, you are a fine poet, and the best surveyor
in Massachusetts, yet you made pencils for a living.

HENRY

Those pencils were an excellent design. I made many
improvements. I will stack my pencils up against any.

WALDO

This is what I'm saying Henry. Anything you do you
do well. And yet what you do is. Well. People don't
understand it.

HENRY

I don't need them to.

WALDO

And now this. Moving here. Building your cabin. It
makes no sense to anyone.

HENRY

Channing approves.

*Waldo laughs.*

WALDO

Don't tell me you are taking advice from him.
Channing is simply happy he isn't considered the
oddest person in Concord anymore.

HENRY

Is that what I am?

WALDO

Yes, Henry. Yes, you are without doubt the oddest person in a community of very odd people. Channing. Bronson Alcott. His daughter Louisa.

HENRY

Your Aunt Mary.

WALDO

I beg your pardon! Alright, yes. Though I would prefer for her the term exceptional.

HENRY

I would agree.

WALDO

Hawthorne is very odd.

HENRY

Odd? Is that the right word for him?

WALDO

Peculiar?

HENRY

Uncanny?

WALDO

Bizarre?

HENRY

Curious?

WALDO

Weird?

*They pause.*

TOGETHER

Weird.

HENRY

He is from Salem. They are all weird there.

WALDO

His wife Sophia[24] is from Salem also.

HENRY

Well. Perhaps not all.

WALDO

Another exceptional.

HENRY

Jones Very.

WALDO

He is not from here.

HENRY

He is of here.

WALDO

True. Poor Jones Very.

HENRY

Too much prophesy in his poetry.

WALDO

And yet the sanest mad man I ever met.

---

[24] Pronounced with a long I. So-Fy-Uh

HENRY

Harvard will do that to you. Speaking of, Willie
Goodwin.

WALDO

You think? I have some hopes for him.

HENRY

And then of course there is you.

WALDO

Me? I am not odd.

HENRY

Ha!

WALDO

I am not. I am normal. I am average. I simply think
and read and write more than other people.

HENRY

You think that is not odd?

WALDO

I am the opposite of odd. With me it is simply too
much normal. Which is why I attract so many odd
people. They find me, like opposite poles.

HENRY

Like gravity. We all circle around you, but never
approach, lest we burn up in the fire of your mind.

WALDO

Hardly. It sounds good though.

HENRY
Is that why I came to you?

WALDO
I couldn't say. Could you?

*Henry is silent for a moment.*

HENRY
You never told me what you thought of it.

WALDO
Thought of what?

HENRY
My essay on Carlyle.

WALDO
Ah. Well done. I said so.

HENRY
Exactly. You shook my hand. You said I did well. But you never said what you thought.

WALDO
That is unusual for me.

HENRY
One might even say odd.

WALDO
One might. Well, it is difficult for me to judge. You know only the words. I know the man.

HENRY
Does that make a difference? It was his words I was writing about.

WALDO
It is hard for me to be objective.

HENRY
Why?

WALDO
The man is a friend.

HENRY
You can't be objective because he is a friend?

WALDO
I don't know.

HENRY
Are you objective with me?

WALDO
It is not the same.

HENRY
You have no trouble criticizing me. You and Margaret
Fuller made something of a sport of it.

WALDO
The pieces you sent to the Dial, they, we, wanted to
help. We see so much promise in you Henry.

HENRY
You keep saying that. Of course I know that, Mr.
Emerson. I am grateful, to you and to Miss Fuller.

WALDO
We want to see the remarkable abilities we know you
possess reach fullness. Maturity.

HENRY
As do I. Why do you think I came out here?

WALDO
I haven't the slightest idea.

HENRY
Don't you?

WALDO
Didn't you like staying with us Henry?

HENRY
Of course I did. You know I did.

WALDO
I thought you did. Everything was in its right place.
Everything worked.

HENRY
For you.

WALDO
But not for you?

HENRY
It was not my place. It was not my home. It was not
my. Family.

WALDO
We all cared for you Henry. The children. Mrs.
Emerson.

HENRY
I know. I.

*Henry stops. He is getting into dangerous territory.*

HENRY

So? What did you think of my lecture?

WALDO

I wish you had left me out of it.

HENRY

How? How can I leave you out of anything. You are Ralph Waldo Emerson.

WALDO

The man who is banished forever from Harvard Divinity School.

HENRY

The American Plato.

WALDO

The man who is foolish enough to spend his life writing and thinking. Usually in that order.

HENRY

The successor to Montaigne. The genius of Concord.

*Henry pauses.*

HENRY

Genius.

*Waldo speaks immediately, impatient with the game now.*

WALDO

In every work of genius we recognize our own
rejected thoughts.[25]

HENRY

You're quoting yourself.

WALDO

It's hard not to.

HENRY

It breaks the rules.

WALDO

Were there rules?

*Henry stares.*

WALDO

Fine.

*Waldo stares back, discerning.*

WALDO

At first glance he measured his companion, and,
though insensible to some fine traits of culture, could
very well report his weight and caliber. And this made
the impression of genius which his conversation
sometimes gave.[26]

---

[25] Emerson, Self-Reliance
[26] Emerson, *Tribute* to Thoreau, Atlantic Magazine, 1862

HENRY

It takes a man of genius to travel in his own country, in his native village; to make any progress between his door and his gate.[27]

*Waldo shakes his head, tired of the game.*

WALDO

I cannot judge.

HENRY

You cannot not. You are everywhere for me. Except here. In this cabin.

WALDO

Except that I am here.

HENRY

But at least I am also here. I am myself here. This is my place. This pond is my pond. These beans are my beans. And I am finding my way here. To something different.

WALDO

Different from me you mean.

HENRY

There is only one Ralph Waldo Emerson.

*Long pause.*

WALDO

How are the beans this year?

---

[27] Thoreau, Journal 1851

HENRY

The late freeze took the crop. Until then I expected 12 bushels.

WALDO

Fertilizer?

HENRY

None. Except the mold left over from the stumps when I pulled them.

WALDO

Economical.

HENRY

Of necessity.

*Waldo looks slyly at Henry.*

WALDO

Necessity.

*Pause.*

HENRY

The better part of the man is soon plowed into the soil for compost. By a seeming fate, commonly called necessity, they are employed, as it says in an old book, laying up treasures which moth and rust will corrupt and thieves break through and steal.[28]

---

[28] Thoreau, *Walden*

WALDO

We are sure, that, though we know not how, necessity does comport with liberty, the individual with the world, my polarity with the spirit of the times.[29]

*They pause. Henry laughs.*

HENRY

You.

*Waldo nods.*

WALDO

Henry.

HENRY

Of necessity.

*Waldo walks around the cabin, inspecting.*

WALDO

The cabin is holding up well.

HENRY

You have not visited in a while, Mr. Emerson.

WALDO

I didn't wish to disturb your work. You said you were making progress.

HENRY

I was. I am. I think.

---

[29] Emerson, *Fate*

*Henry pauses.*

WALDO
How much longer do you plan to stay?

HENRY
That is up to you.

WALDO
How do you mean?

HENRY
This is your land.

WALDO
Henry. Please. I don't wish to argue. At least not about that.

HENRY
We are who we are.

WALDO
As you say. I wanted you to know that I am going away.

HENRY
West? South?

WALDO
East. Back to Europe.

HENRY
How long?

WALDO
Six months this time. Possibly longer.

*Pause.*

HENRY

When?

WALDO

September.

HENRY

Impossible. What of your trees sir?

WALDO

My orchard you mean?

HENRY

You may possibly get in your peaches by then, the
Early Rose and the Presidents. And your pears may
well be fine, the Seckels and the Bloodgoods certainly.
But what of your apples? The Gravensteins, the
Bellflowers and the Hightops? And the quince. Don't
get me started on the quince.

WALDO

I have been very concerned about the quince. You
know I love my quince apple pie. Mrs. Emerson's pies
are the wonder of New England.

HENRY

I remember.

WALDO

So I thought. I was hoping. We all, the family, you see,
were hoping. The orchard has never fared so well as
when you were tending it, Henry.

HENRY

No.

WALDO

Your apple needs you Henry. The one you grew, the one we named for you. The Thoreau is wasting away in your absence.

HENRY

I have my work here.

WALDO

I don't understand this choice, Henry. When you asked to build out here, I agreed. But I didn't understand. I still don't.

HENRY

My work is here.

WALDO

You are a talented poet.

HENRY

I'm not a poet. I don't know what I am but it isn't a poet.

WALDO

Then write something else.

HENRY

I'm trying.

WALDO

Solitude is necessary. I understand that. But isolation? For one with your temperament. Is that wise?

*Henry pauses.*

        HENRY

Wisdom.

        WALDO

Henry.

        HENRY

Wisdom.

        WALDO

Can't we?

        HENRY

Wisdom.

        WALDO

To finish the moment, to find the journey's end in every step of the road, to live the greatest number of good hours, is wisdom.[30]

        HENRY

How insufficient is all wisdom without love[31].

*Neither speaks for a moment.*

        WALDO

The children miss you Henry.

        HENRY

I still see them.

---

[30] Emerson, *Experience*
[31] Thoreau, *Journals*

WALDO
Mrs. Emerson misses you.

HENRY
I miss them all.

WALDO
Then come home, Henry.

HENRY
It isn't my home. I will never have a home. Not in that sense. Nor wife. Nor children. I know that now. It is not a life meant for me. Or a life I wasn't meant for.

WALDO
You don't have to make that choice. I know there is a pressure. Yes there are compromises. Distractions. Interruptions certainly. From the work we do. But they are necessary. I don't know how to say it. I'm not speaking of love.

HENRY
Don't, sir.

WALDO
A life together. Children. The things they teach you. The foundation they give you.

HENRY
I saw that foundation crumble.

*Waldo pauses, sinks into a chair.*

HENRY
I loved him too.

WALDO
He was a wondrous child.

HENRY
I saw him suffer just as you did.

WALDO
My deep-eyed boy.

HENRY
I saw him die.

WALDO
My Waldo.

HENRY
The same year.

WALDO
I know.

HENRY
The same year.

WALDO
I'm sorry.

HENRY
The same year as John.

WALDO
Your brother was. We all.

HENRY
Waldo from scarlet fever and John from lockjaw.

WALDO
I have never left that room. I am still holding him.

HENRY
Five years ago.

WALDO
Is it five?

HENRY
The year your essays were published. I don't know how you managed it. I don't know. How.

WALDO
It's what we do.

HENRY
It is. Yes.

WALDO
It's what we must do.

HENRY
It's what I am doing.

WALDO
Necessity.

HENRY
You see what you invite me back to.

WALDO
My boy. Can't you see that...

HENRY
No. It is not that way, with us. That's not who we are.

WALDO
Are you sure?

HENRY

I have loved.

WALDO

It's not important.

HENRY

I have loved.

WALDO

Yes yes.

HENRY

I still love.

WALDO

Mrs. Emerson.

*Henry turns quickly.*

HENRY

Sir?

WALDO

Mrs. Emerson. She would.

HENRY

Yes.

WALDO

She wished me to ask.

HENRY

Yes.

WALDO

Mrs. Emerson would like some beans. If there are any left. That is what I came to ask.

HENRY

Really?

WALDO

She would take me to task if I forgot.

HENRY

For.

WALDO

You know Lidian.

HENRY

I know. Mrs. Emerson.

*Henry pauses. Deciding.*

HENRY

What I have, I'll bring.

WALDO

I know you will. I don't understand, Henry. But I do trust.

*Waldo hands the papers back to Henry, then starts to leave. He stops at the door.*

WALDO

Henry.

HENRY

Yes, Mr. Emerson?

WALDO
I am not objective.

HENRY
Sir?

WALDO
About you. I am not objective about you.

*Henry waits.*

WALDO
I believe that I am less objective about you than any friend I have ever had.

HENRY
I'll keep that in mind, Mr. Emerson.

WALDO
Do please, Mr. Thoreau.

*Waldo walks through the door. Looks around.*

WALDO
Good spot for a cabin. I hope it lasts.

*Lights fade.*

**The End**

STEPHEN EVANS

# Tender

STEPHEN EVANS

# The History

"A true friend is this tender, illustrious man."

Louisa May Alcott,
*Journal Entry*

In January of 1842, Ralph Waldo Emerson's son Waldo fell ill with scarlet fever. Five days later, he died.

As Lousia May Alcott later described that day, her father and Emerson's close friend Bronson Alcott sent Louisa to see how the young boy was doing. When Emerson opened the door, she explained her errand. "He is dead, child," Emerson said, and closed the door.

This play imagines a different scenario, in which both Emerson's protégé Henry David Thoreau and Emerson's grieving wife Lidian have parts to play.

From a young age, Louisa was a frequent visitor to the Emerson household, had looked after the children Waldo and Ellen, and was infatuated by the two very different men, both of whom were to influence her life and writing.

# Cast of Characters

LOUISA        Louisa May Alcott, Age 9

WALDO         Ralph Waldo Emerson, Age 39

HENRY         Henry David Thoreau, Age 25

LIDIAN/       Lidian Emerson, Age 40

## Scene

Emerson's study in Concord.

## Time

January 28, 1842.

STEPHEN EVANS

# ACT I SCENE 1

**Setting:** Ralph Waldo Emerson's study is a small well-appointed room. A round table in the middle of the room is piled with books.

**At Rise:** Waldo is at the table, struggling to light an oil lamp.

*Louisa enters quietly, waits for a moment, somewhat in awe and reluctant to disturb him.*

LOUISA
Excuse me, Mr. Emerson.

*Waldo looks up, pauses, as if searching for a name.*

WALDO
Louisa.

LOUISA
Sir, my father sent me to ask about little Waldo.

*Waldo pauses again, as if she is speaking a language he cannot understand. Then he blows out the match.*

WALDO

He is dead, child.

*Louisa doesn't respond. Waldo gets up and shuffles her kindly away towards the door. He turns back to the desk.*

WALDO

Tell Mr. Alcott I will write to him.

*Louisa stands a moment, trembling, turns to leave, then collapses.*

WALDO

Louisa!

*Waldo rushes to her.*

WALDO

I am sorry, child.

*He helps her to a chair.*

WALDO

Henry!

*Henry enters.*

WALDO

Henry, would you bring Louisa some water? She is feeling unsteady.

*He looks at Louisa, nods, and quickly leaves.*

WALDO

He doesn't say much, our Henry. At the best of times.
Which this is not.

LOUISA

You shall miss him.

WALDO

The old should not survive the young.

LOUISA

Are you very old? My father is.

WALDO

Your father is wise. That makes him seem old.

*Henry enters with water, hands the cup to
Louisa, then leaves.*

LOUISA

He is sad.

WALDO

He loved my son. He was so good about spending
time with him. They would wander through the
orchard for hours sometimes, and Henry would
explain all about the trees and the fruit, which were
sweet, which were tart, which made the best pies.
Waldo was curious about everything. And he loved
pies, like his father.

LOUISA

His brother died. Lockjaw, my father said.

                    WALDO
Henry's brother John. Yes. Tragic. Just recently he
made a remarkable daguerreotype of Waldo. To
lose them both.

    *Waldo pauses, lost in thought.*

                    LOUISA
Are you sad?

    *Waldo pauses again, thinking.*

                    WALDO
I am sure I will be.

    *Louisa thinks about that.*

                    LOUISA
I am sad.

    *Lidian enters, watching from the doorway.*

                    WALDO
It is right to be sad when something beautiful passes
away.

                    LOUISA
Waldo was so lovely and good. He always minded
when I watched him. I shall miss him.

                    WALDO
Will you?

    *She nods.*

LOUISA
He is with God now.

*At this Waldo starts to break. He gathers
himself, almost as if beginning a lecture, and
starts to speak. Lidian strides in, furious.*

LIDIAN.
Don't you dare. Don't you dare, Mr. Emerson. Don't
you tell her my son is not in Heaven. Don't you dare
tell her that.

*She can't continue. Waldo gets up and walks to
her. They look at each other, do not touch.*

WALDO
Henry!

*Henry enters. Waldo's eyes do not leave Lidian.*

WALDO
Henry, will you see Louisa home?

HENRY.
Of course, Mr. Emerson.

*Waldo takes Lidian's arm. She pulls away. He
rests a hand gently on her shoulder and guides
her out of the room. Before leaving, he stops and
turns to Louisa.*

WALDO
Wherever he is, I believe that God is with him.

LOUISA
Well. That's alright then.

*Waldo and Lidian leave. Henry sits on the floor near Louisa. She takes a sip of water. They are silent for a moment.*

LOUISA
He has wonderful books, doesn't he?

HENRY
Yes.

*Louisa stands.*

*Thoreau looks at her sharply, ready to brace her if she falls. But she seems fine. He relaxes.*

LOUISA
He lets me borrow them sometimes.

*She walks to the table, examining the books.*

LOUISA
And sometimes I read the ones he sends to my father.

HENRY
That's good, Louisa.

LOUISA
My father believes that even girls deserve an education.

HENRY
I agree with him. Your father is a wise man.

LOUISA

So everyone says. He teaches us himself. In our home.

*She picks up a book, glances through it.*

LOUISA

I have even read Mr. Emerson's book.

*Henry looks up at this, amused.*

HENRY

What did you think?

*She puts the book back.*

LOUISA

He quotes from other writers too often. A good writer shouldn't need to quote others. He should say what he has to say himself.

HENRY

I'll keep that in mind.

*She picks up another book, weighs it in her hand, puts it back.*

LOUISA

Too heavy. Books shouldn't be too heavy. They should be light enough to carry around in one's pocket.

HENRY

I'll keep that in mind too. Any more advice for writers?

LOUISA
Don't be boring.

*Henry rises and walks to the table, checking the books himself.*

LOUISA
I shall write about pirates I think.

HENRY
Do you know any pirates?

LOUISA
Not yet. But I am only nine. So far.

HENRY
You have time.

LOUISA
I hope so. Waldo didn't.

HENRY
No.

LOUISA
I had a brother.

HENRY
You did?

LOUISA
He died. But still.

HENRY
Yes. Still.

LOUISA
I have three sisters.

HENRY
You could write about them.

LOUISA
Too boring.

HENRY
I think sometimes boring books are the ones people most need to read.

LOUISA
Like what?

HENRY
I don't know. What is the most boring thing you can think of?

*She thinks,*

LOUISA
Beans.

HENRY
Beans?

LOUISA
Father says it is wrong to eat meat. So we eat a lot of beans. They are very boring.

HENRY
Beans. Hmmm.

LOUISA
I bet pirates don't eat beans.

HENRY
Beans keep very well on a sea voyage.

LOUISA
My pirates won't eat beans.

*Waldo enters.*

HENRY
All writing is making choices. Or so I have been told.

WALDO
All life is making choices. Unless they are made for you. Henry. Mrs. Emerson is asking for you.

HENRY
For me?

WALDO
Perhaps you will have more luck in comforting her. I don't seem to have that skill.

HENRY
Of course.

*He leaves.*

WALDO
Louisa, Henry will walk you home a bit later. Is that all right? I shall write a note to your father explaining.

WALDO
Yes Mr. Emerson.

*Waldo goes to his table and starts writing.*
*Louisa moves quietly to the table and watches*
*him.*

LOUISA
Mr. Emerson?

*Not looking up.*

WALDO
Yes Louisa?

LOUISA
Shall I go in and see to Ellen?

WALDO
No dear.

LOUISA
I have cared for her before.

WALDO
Yes I remember. You are an excellent nurse. Perhaps
that shall be your career.

LOUISA
Can you make money at it?

WALDO
I suppose a bit. Do you need money?

LOUISA
Our family always seems to.

WALDO
That is certainly true.

*He folds a note and hands it to Louisa, who places it carefully in a pocket. Waldo selects another piece of paper and continues writing.*

LOUISA
Why is that?

WALDO
Pardon?

LOUISA
If my father is so wise, why do we never have any money? Can't wise people make money?

WALDO
Not usually. No. Most people who are wise are also poor.

LOUISA
Why is that?

WALDO
Because I suppose they have better things to do than make money.

LOUISA
Are you wise?

WALDO
Not today.

LOUISA
Are you poor?

WALDO
Not if I finish this essay.

*Louisa moves to stand behind Waldo and looks at the paper.*

LOUISA
You can make money from writing?

WALDO
Only if you finish it.

LOUISA
I shall be a writer then.

WALDO
Good for you, dear.

LOUISA
I shall write about pirates. Who don't eat beans.

*Waldo looks up at her. She moves off, wandering around the room. He goes back to writing.*

WALDO
I don't believe I have ever read anything like that.

LOUISA
I shall be an original.

WALDO
Like your father.

LOUISA
I shall be an original who makes money.

WALDO
An excellent plan.

LOUISA

It is.

WALDO

You are surrounded by originals. You have met my friend Ms. Fuller, I believe. She is another original.

LOUISA

She talks too.

WALDO

Pardon?

LOUISA

Like my father. She hosts Conversations. Can you make money talking?

WALDO

Sometimes. Politicians seem to do quite well. But I don't think you can be one.

LOUISA

Why not?

WALDO

You can't vote.

LOUISA

Why not?

WALDO

You can't own property.

LOUISA

Who says so?

WALDO

The laws of Massachusetts say so.

LOUISA
Who makes the laws?

WALDO
Politicians.

LOUISA
Who are men.

WALDO
Exactly.

LOUISA
It all seems very suspicious to me.

WALDO
I suppose it is. But perhaps you will feel different
when you are married.

LOUISA
Oh I shall never marry.

*Waldo looks up.*

WALDO
Why is that?

LOUISA
My father needs me.

WALDO
Daughters are a comfort to their fathers. But you may
feel differently when you are older.

LOUISA
I might. I doubt he will.

*Waldo studies her a moment.*

WALDO
You remind me of someone.

LOUISA
Who?

WALDO
I can't remember. Louisa, perhaps you could ask cook
to make a cup of tea, and then you could bring it to
Mrs. Emerson. She might find it a comfort.

LOUISA
Yes Mr. Emerson.

*Louisa starts to go, then stops.*

LOUISA
Why don't you?

WALDO
Pardon?

LOUISA
You wished to comfort Mrs. Emerson, and you think a
cup of tea would be comforting. Why don't you bring
it to her?

WALDO
That is something else you will understand when you
are married.

LOUISA
I have said I shall not marry, so perhaps you should
explain it to me now.

WALDO

Henry.

LOUISA

Where?

WALDO

That is who you remind me of. Henry.

LOUISA

I don't think we look much alike. He is older. And
almost has a beard.

WALDO

So he does. I merely mean that he has an endless
supply of questions.

LOUISA

They are only endless because no one gives me the
answers.

WALDO

No one ever gives answers, Louisa. They always come
at a cost.

*Louisa digs in her pocket and puts some coins on
the desk.*

LOUISA

Three cents worth please.

*Waldo smiles, then sighs. He starts to break,
then collects himself.*

WALDO

I don't know that I have so many today.

LOUISA

Mr. Emerson, you are said to be a very fine explainer. Will you not explain to me why a cup of tea from me is comforting and a cup from you is not? I believe this could be very important to my future happiness.

*Waldo picks up the coins.*

WALDO

For three pennies, I shall give you three answers. Is that fair?

*He holds up one penny.*

First, because you are not her husband and she is not your wife.

*He holds up the second penny.*

Second, because I am her husband, and she is my wife.

*He holds up the third penny.*

Third, because I am her first husband, and she is my second wife.

*Louisa thinks.*

LOUISA

I should like my three cents back.

WALDO

I don't blame you.

*He gives them back.*

LOUISA

Families are very complicated in my opinion.

*Waldo begins writing again.*

WALDO

Perhaps that is what you should write about.

*Louisa thinks.*

LOUISA

I suppose pirates have families.

WALDO

I'm sure they do.

LOUISA

I still don't understand why you aren't sad. Mrs.
Emerson is sad. I am sad. Mr. Thoreau is sad. Why
aren't you?

*Waldo thinks for a moment.*

WALDO

Because I am broken.

LOUISA

What does that mean? You are Mr. Emerson. How can
you be broken?

WALDO

My father died when I was your age. My wife, Ellen,
the first Ellen, died when we had been just few
months married. My brother Edward passed shortly
after. Then Charles. Charles. You are too young to
remember him. Charles was the real genius of the
Emerson family. He was another original.

*He pauses.*

LOUISA
I'm sorry.

WALDO
When that is your life. Loss after loss after loss. And when you are a particular kind of person, a particular kind of man. Something in you breaks. Your heart disconnects. And you are left alone in your mind. Forever.

LOUISA
That sounds awful.

WALDO
It is. But because of it I can do a few things that other people find difficult.

LOUISA
So it is a cost.

WALDO
Yes. That I try and make the best of.

LOUISA
And Mrs. Emerson is not broken. So she can be sad.

WALDO
Mrs. Emerson is. The best woman. The best wife.

LOUISA
I don't think I will get married. Not even to a pirate. Father and mother adore each other and are miserable. You and Mrs. Emerson—

WALDO

You are a very perceptive child, Louisa. That may not lead you to a happy life.

LOUISA

Are there any?

*Henry enters.*

HENRY

Mr. Emerson, Ellen has a fever also.

WALDO

What? No.

*He gets up to go.*

WALDO

Henry, please see Louisa home.

HENRY

Of course.

WALDO

Then come right back. She will need you.

*Waldo starts to leave.*

LOUISA

Mr. Emerson?

*He stops.*

LOUISA

You comfort me.

*Waldo is moved.*

WALDO
Thank you, Louisa.

*He turns to go, turns back.*

WALDO
You should write about families, Louisa. Just not mine.

*Lights fade.*

**The End**

# Bibliography

## Plutarch:

*The Morals*, by Plutarch, corrected and revised by William W. Goodwin, Ph. D. 1870

## Emerson Biographies:

My favorites among many:

*Emerson: The Mind on Fire* by Robert D. Richardson Jr.

*Ralph Waldo Emerson* by Oliver Wendell Holmes Sr.

## Emerson Correspondence:

*Letters of Ellen Tucker Emerson*, edited by Edith W. Gregg

*Letters of Ralph Waldo Emerson*, edited by Ralph L. Rusk

*One First Love, The Letters of Ellen Luisa Tucker to Ralph Waldo Emerson,* edited by Edith W. Gregg

## Emerson's Works:

Most of Emerson's own works, as well as those of Henry David Thoreau and Louisa May Alcott, are in print and/or available online.

STEPHEN EVANS

# Acknowledgements

The original version of *Monuments* opened as part of the play *Generations* on August 2, 2019, at Colonial Players in Annapolis, Maryland. The play was directed by Lois Evans and starred Jeffrey Miller and Kate Wheeler.

Generations also included the one-act plays *Last Laugh* by Morey Norkin and *Late Nights in Cars* by Michael Gilles.

The world premiere reading of *Solid Seasons* occurred in Concord, Massachusetts, at the 2023 Thoreau Society Annual Gathering.

I am grateful to the Thoreau Society, which sponsored the event, and to Mr. Brent Ranalli, who offered helpful suggestions and read the part of Henry David Thoreau.

# Books by Stephen Evans

## Plays:

*The Visitation Quartet:*
   *The Ghost Writer*
   *Monuments*
   *Tourists*
   *Spooky Action at a Distance*

*At the Still Point*

| | |
|---|---|
| *Experience* | *Three plays about Ralph Waldo Emerson* |
| *Generations* | *(with Morey Norkin and Michael Gilles)* |
| *As You Like It* | *(by William Shakespeare, adapted by Stephen Evans)* |
| *The Glass Door* | *(An adaptation of Hedda Gabler by Henrik Ibsen)* |

## Non-Fiction:

*Funny Thing Is:*    *A Guide to Understanding Comedy*
*Anthropomorphosis*
*Small Gifts*
*Liebestraum*
*The Laughing String: Thoughts on Writing*

## Fiction:

*The Marriage of True Minds*
*The Island of Always:*
*The Marriage Gift*
*Whose Beauty is Past Change*
*The Mind of a Writer and other Fables*
*Memory Plays*
*Epigrammaticon*
*The Next Joy and the Next*

## Verse:

*Limerosity*
*Limerositus*
*Sonets from the Chesapeke*
*The Crooked Mirror*

STEPHEN EVANS

www.ingramcontent.com/pod-product-compliance
Lightning Source LLC
Chambersburg PA
CBHW021649120626
46545CB00002B/771